Bookclub-in-a-Box presents the discussion companion for Paula McLain's novel

The Paris Wife

Novel published in hardcover by Bond Street Books, a registered trademark of Random House of Canada, 2011.

ISBN: 978-0-385-66922-1

Quotations used in this guide have been taken from the text of the hardcover edition of *The Paris Wife*. All information taken from other sources is acknowledged.

This discussion companion was written by Marilyn Herbert, B.Ed. She is the founder of Bookclub-in-a-Box and an international speaker with more than 30 years experience as a teacher and school librarian. Bookclub-in-a-Box is a unique guide to current fiction and classic literature intended for book club discussions, educational study seminars, and personal pleasure.

This guide was co-written by Samantha Bailey, with assistance by Graeme Bayliss. For more information about the Bookclub-in-a-Box team, visit our website.

Bookclub-in-a-Box discussion companion for

The Paris Wife

(PRINT) ISBN: 978-1-927121-00-9
(E-PUB) ISBN: 978-1-927121-01-6
(E-PDF) ISBN: 978-1-927121-02-3

This guide reflects the perspective of the Bookclub-in-a-Box team and is the sole property of Bookclub-in-a-Box.

BOOKCLUB-IN-A-BOX
Paula McLain's The Paris Wife

BOOKCLUB-IN-A-BOX
Readers and Leaders Guide

Each Bookclub-in-a-Box guide is clearly and effectively organized to give you information and ideas for a lively discussion, as well as to present the major highlights of the novel. The format, with a Table of Contents, allows you to pick and choose the specific points you wish to talk about. It does not have to be used in any prescribed order. In fact, it is meant to support, not determine, your discussion.

You Choose What to Use.

You may find that some information is repeated in more than one section and may be cross-referenced so as to provide insight on the same idea from different angles.

The guide is formatted to give you extra space to make your own notes.

How to Begin

Relax and look forward to enjoying your book club.

With Bookclub-in-a-Box as your behind the scenes support, there is little for you to do in the way of preparation.

Some readers like to review the guide after reading the novel; some before. Either way, the guide is all you will need as a companion for your discussion. You may find that the guide's interpretation, information, and background have sparked other ideas not included.

Having read the novel and armed with Bookclub-in-a-Box, you will be well prepared to lead or guide or listen to the discussion at hand.

Lastly, if you need some more "hands on" support, feel free to contact us.

What to Look For

Each Bookclub-in-a-Box guide is divided into easy-to-use sections, which include points on characters, themes, writing style and structure, literary or historical background, author information, and other pertinent features unique to the novel being discussed. These may vary slightly from guide to guide.

INTERPRETATION OF EACH NOVEL REFLECTS THE PERSPECTIVE OF THE BOOKCLUB-IN-A-BOX TEAM.

Do We Need to Agree?

THE ANSWER TO THIS QUESTION IS NO.

If we have sparked a discussion or a debate on certain points, then we are happy. We invite you to share your group's alternative findings and experiences. You can contact us via our website (www.bookclubinabox.com), by email (info@bookclubinabox.com), or by phone (1-866-578-5571). We would love to hear from you.

Discussion Starters

There are as many ways to begin a book club discussion as there are members in your group. If you are an experienced group, you will already have your favorite ways to begin. If you are a newly formed group or a group looking for new ideas, here are some suggestions.

- Ask for people's impressions of the novel. (This will give you some idea about which parts of the unit to focus on.)
- Identify a favorite or major character.
- Identify a favorite or major idea.
- Begin with a powerful or pertinent quote. (Not necessarily from the novel.)
- Discuss the historical information of the novel. (Not applicable to all novels.)
- If this author is familiar to the group, discuss the range of his/her work and where this novel stands in that range.
- Use the discussion topics and questions in the Bookclub-in-a-Box guide.

If you have further suggestions for discussion starters, be sure to share them with us and we will share them with others.

Above All, Enjoy Yourselves

INTRODUCTION

Novel Quickline

Key to the Novel

Author Information

INTRODUCTION

Novel Quickline

1920 was the start of a new and exciting decade. The First World War had just ended, and life was changing for both men and women. Despite America's prohibition era, life seemed more free than ever. Hidden inside the speak-easies and private homes, people celebrated life and living. They drank and danced their way into forgetting the torment of the previous decade of war.

Under the lights of this American stage, 29-year-old Hadley Richardson met a dynamic and intense 21-year-old Ernest Hemingway and they fell in love. The story of their romance and subsequent marriage is captured in *The Paris Wife*, a novel based on the true story of Hemingway's first wife.

As the pages turn, Hadley engages us in her life with Ernest until both the marriage and the story draw to a heartwrenching close.

Key to the Novel

In Paula McLain's novel, Ernest Hemingway is not yet a famous writer and we are treated to a personal perspective of the man behind the iconic persona, as told by the primary woman in his life at the time: the young and innocent Hadley Richardson. She is Hemingway's first wife during his sojourn in Paris.

The novel's style and structure is the successful key that unlocks Hadley's story. While it is Hadley's voice we hear throughout, McLain often uses Hemingway's strong and simple writing style to contain that voice. By using Hadley's words and thoughts, McLain shows how completely overwhelmed she was by her husband, to the point where she submerged her own interests, struggles, and passions in favor of his.

The evolution of Hadley Richardson from being Ernest Hemingway's first wife to becoming a woman of her own is McLain's remarkable achievement. She places Hadley as the lead character in her husband's life and work. **(see Writing Style and Structure, p.41)**

Author Information

- Before this book, Paula McLain already had experience in the field of memoir-writing. Not only has she written *The Paris Wife* (2010), the memoir-style novel about Ernest Hemingway's first wife, but she has written her own real memoir, *Like Family: Growing Up in Other People's Houses* (2003).

- McLain was born in 1965, the second of three sisters in Fresno, California. In 1970, the girls were abandoned by their parents. Dad was in jail for robbery, and Mom disappeared with a boyfriend. Until McLain was 18 years old, she and her siblings lived in a series of foster homes, some good and others not. It was only the last foster home, belonging to Bub and Hilde Lindbergh, that they stayed in for 11 years. The three sisters did not remain close to or even in touch with the Lindberghs afterwards, but they felt that this house was the closest thing they had to a home. The important thing was that the girls were together.

- Both of McLain's sisters are married with children, as is McLain herself; the author now lives with her family in Cleveland, Ohio. The sisters are still close and their mother is now back in their lives, remarried for the fifth time. However, their mother still has problems with a fragile state of mind.

- In the author's memoir, there is a tone of being removed and somewhat distant from her mother. It is as if she is looking at her past life through a smudged glass-pane window. Given her personal history, there is a degree of honest and raw emotion that comes through Hadley in relation to McLain's own family story. Both women had difficulties with their mothers, as did Hemingway.

Although there are many differences between Paula McLain and her subject, Hadley Richardson, what similarities (if any) might they share?

- McLain always wanted to be a writer, but she struggled to find a publisher for *The Paris Wife*. Her previous publisher did not feel that the novel would be successful, and she claims she was down to her last few dollars when Random House took a chance and published the book. Its success ensures that McLain is free to continue writing fiction for some time to come.

CHARACTERIZATION

Hadley Richardson

Ernest Hemingway

Gertrude Stein

Ezra Pound

F. Scott and Zelda Fitzgerald

The Murphys and the MacLeishes

Chink

Kate Smith

Kitty Cannell and Harold Loeb

Pauline Pfeiffer

CHARACTERIZATION

Paula McLain has written a book based on real events and real people, including some of the greatest writers and thinkers in literary history. Ezra Pound, Gertrude Stein, Alice B. Toklas, James Joyce, and Zelda and F. Scott Fitzgerald figure heavily in the novel. These literary and artistic giants are relatable because of how Hadley interacts with them. In McLain's novel, these real people are characters in Hadley's drama and will be described as such for the purposes of this guide.

While the basic details and particulars for each of the main characters are factual, the portraits are composites drawn from McLain's research and imagination. How do these portraits match or contrast your own knowledge of these literary stars?

Hadley Richardson

- Hadley is shaped by her experiences with the people and events around her. McLain shows her background to be a solidly moneyed middle-class. Hadley's paternal grandfather established the Richardson Drug Company, which her father continued to run, and her maternal grandfather founded a number of schools. Her parents appear as opposites. Her dad was soft, sad, and quiet, while her mother was outspoken and opinionated. It seemed that her father drank quietly and largely tried to keep out of her mother's way.

- Hadley's childhood was difficult in a number of ways, bordering on the tragic. She was one of four children, born in two separate groupings. The older siblings were Jamie and Dorothea, while her sister, Fonnie, was the closest to her in age and companionship.

- Born a strong-willed adventurer, Hadley's sense of self was stifled by her family after she had an accident. She was six when a mishap occurred and she fell out of an upper storey window, leaving her bedridden for months. Deprived of the normal childhood activities like swimming, running, and playing, Hadley missed a lot of school due to her fall and so she wasn't ready to go off to college with her friends. She fell out of step with them and was, consequently, less confident and more vulnerable than they were. Hadley became an obsessive reader and found her pleasure in books. Perhaps that was one reason she became so strongly attracted to Ernest.

- By the time she is a young adult, she is essentially alone, having lost her closest family members to tragic circumstances. Her father commits suicide, her beloved sister, Dorothea, dies in a horrible accident, and her mother succumbs to a lengthy and painful illness. Her sister, Fonnie, is the only family member at hand, but they are no longer as close as they were as children. Sadness continues to surround Hadley as Fonnie's marriage falls apart and Roland, Fonnie's husband, descends into mental instability.

- Suppressed by dark thoughts and dreams, Hadley feels as though she has been caught in a *"kind of coma for eight ... years."* (p.30) At 28 years of age, Hadley is finally ready to throw herself open to life.

Despite her age, Hadley has had almost no experience with romance, or even friendships, with men. If Hadley hadn't met Ernest at this very vulnerable time, would she have sought out other

adventure? Was she inhibited by the times in which she lived or by her own nature?

- Hadley falls passionately in love, and her own dreams of playing piano are forgotten as she spends her life supporting Ernest and his quest to be a published writer.

- Following Ernest to France, Spain, Toronto, Switzerland, and Germany, Hadley never quite fits in with Ernest's colorful and exciting group of friends. Artistic legends, fashionistas, and literary stars are an integral part of Ernest's inner circle. Hadley doesn't have her own friends, nor her own interests. She does not appear to be self-aware until much later in the novel.

- McLain's Hadley is warm, personable, and charming. Introverted in some circumstances, she tries to keep up with Ernest.

  At the beginning of each evening, I was nervous and shy, worried that I had nothing to contribute to the group, but then I'd settle into my skin and my voice. By midnight, I would be part of things, ready to drink like a sailor and talk until morning. It was like being born over each night, the same process repeated, finding myself, losing myself, finding myself again. (p.44)

- Perhaps subconsciously to gain some control over her life, she does things that unwittingly stymie Ernest's success. She accidentally gets pregnant by leaving her birth control at home while they are away in Chamby; she also packs up every single line of his life's work into a valise, only to leave it on a train.

What are the implications of Hadley's actions? Do these incidents change the direction of their relationship and become a turning point in their marriage? Does her relationship with Pauline fit into this potential theory?

- Pauline, Hadley's close friend, is the woman who influences both her fashion choices and her decision to finally have her own piano concert, a long held dream. As Pauline moves into their lives, she and Ernest begin a convenient affair. Instead of getting angry, Hadley mutes her feelings and her voice in an attempt to keep Ernest by her side.

  > *I must have heard her say 'It's heaven' a thousand times over that summer, until I wanted to scream. I didn't scream, though, and that became one of the things I grew to regret.* (p.279)

- It is this affair that is ultimately the Hemingways' undoing, but Hadley finally regains herself and her life. On an outing to the beach, as Pauline and Ernest jump off a cliff into a swirling tide, Hadley has finally had enough. They want her to jump, and at first, she readies herself. But she suddenly changes her mind and walks away.

  > *When I finally looked down, here were these two wet heads in the slow-moving waves. They looked playful and natural as seals there, and suddenly I knew I wouldn't jump and it had nothing to do with fear or embarrassment. I wouldn't jump because I didn't want to join them.* (p.286)

- Hadley breaks free of the destructiveness of her marriage and some of her friendships and finally discovers that a happy relationship and life is possible. But, sadly, it can only happen for her without Ernest.

- It is fitting that Hadley is a pianist because she plays counterpoint to Hemingway. She and Ernest had hoped that the melodies of their lives would play in sync. But over time, they found themselves more and more in conflict and contrast.

Would an older, wiser, more experienced Hadley have been so attracted to Ernest Hemingway, a man eight years her junior?

We see from McLain's presentation of the young Hadley that, in

choosing Ernest, Hadley was throwing caution to the wind. Was this part of or against her nature? What was in Hemingway's nature that caused him to be so attracted Hadley?

Ernest Hemingway

- McLain's perspective on Hemingway is one not typically seen in other critical biographies and reviews about this master writer. Through Hadley we are treated to a view of Hemingway that shows his youthful innocence and immaturity, his sensitivity, his hopes and dreams before they become tarnished through his experiences in life. When Hadley first sees him, she thinks he radiates happiness. *"There wasn't any fear in him that I could see, just intensity and aliveness. His eyes sparked all over everything ... "* (p.6)

- However, this does not last long. Along with Hadley, we start to see the creation of the legendary Ernest Hemingway, the one who is usually portrayed as a brilliant, self-destructive, and selfish man driven to succeed. Women, for him, are useful as fodder for his writing and to fuel his desires. It becomes clear that his disrespect and intolerance of his mother extends to many women, including perhaps his first wife, Hadley. **(See Women, p.55)**

- Hemingway's parents were similar to Hadley's in some ways, and maybe this was part of their mutual attraction. His father was a doctor and had a good income, while his mother didn't work. She seemed as determined as Hadley's mother to comment on his life. They were not supportive of his writing career and said so in a biting rebuke of his first published work, *Three Stories and Ten Poems*.

From *The Paris Wife*:

> *... Ernest's father [said] he and Grace weren't comfortable having such material in the house. It was vulgar*

and profane at best. They wanted great things for him and hoped he would someday find a way to use his God-given talent to write something with strong morals and virtues. (p.193)

- Hemingway's pain and vulnerability are hidden behind his bravado. Writing is his only true love, and everything he does is for the sole purpose of being published and becoming famous, no matter who he hurts along the way.

- Sherwood Anderson, a mentor and friend, is always willing to help Ernest realize his dream of being published. Perhaps it is envy or anger that propels Ernest to write *Torrents of Spring*, a parody/satire of Sherwood's successful first novel.

- Ernest single-handedly destroys almost every friendship he has by doing exactly what he wants. When Gertrude Stein implores him not to publish *Torrents of Spring* because it is mean-spirited, he dismisses her. He is cruel to Zelda Fitzgerald, F. Scott Fitzgerald's beloved wife, and does not even read Fitzgerald's heralded novel, *The Great Gatsby*, until almost forced to by Hadley.

- He shuts himself away to write, knowing how lonely Hadley is, and travels to exotic locations once they've had their first child, Bumby. Leaving Hadley alone to care for their child, he relentlessly pursues his dream without her.

- Ultimately, Ernest embarks on an affair with Pauline and convinces Hadley, who will do anything for her husband, to allow Pauline to travel and live with them. He strips Hadley of her dreams, her trust, and her self-identity until she has no choice but to leave.

- Alcohol is Ernest's muse and his biggest vice. While he does not die of alcoholism, it certainly contributes to his depression. Although we don't get this far in *The Paris Wife*, Ernest has three more wives after divorcing Hadley and two more sons, but nothing is enough to quiet the pain that has lived inside him. At the age of 61, Ernest Hemingway shoots himself in the head and dies.

What was your impression of Hemingway before reading McLain's novel? What surprised you? What shocked you? What disappointed you?

Supporting Characters

McLain uses Hemingway's relationships to make the point that he was an angry young man. They cannot be called true friendships because they do not grow — instead, they dissolve. This is as true of his marriage to Hadley as it was in his feud with his friend Kenley Smith over back rent.

Gertrude Stein

- Gertrude Stein, a published author and art collector, appears to be the only woman Ernest feels is worthy of his respect. There is no sexual tension, flirting, or wrestling for control. He is desperate to impress her, but then he systematically destroys their friendship. Stein hates his parody of Sherwood Anderson in *Torrents of Spring*. The negative responses from his other friends, Stein included, seems to stoke his desire to have it published. With this act, Ernest ultimately pushes away Anderson, his first mentor, and truly, the writer who taught him his iconic style.

Given Hemingway's general attitude to women, why do you think he relates to Stein differently from other women?

Ezra Pound

- In the beginning, Hemingway defers to Ezra Pound as a student would to a beloved and revered tutor: *"Ernest was literally crouched at Pound's feet while the older man lectured, waving a teapot around as he talked."* (p.85) Hemingway is impressed by the depth and shape of Pound's ideas, encouraged by Pound's interest in his work, and influenced by Pound's strange and open marital relationship with Shakespear.

- Pound set Hemingway's thinking in the direction of his "iceberg" theory of writing. *"Cut everything superfluous ... Go in fear of abstractions. Don't tell readers what to think. Let the action speak for itself."* (p.89) (see Iceberg Theory, p.46)

- Hemingway not only absorbs Pound's literary philosophies, but is also influenced by Ezra Pound's character and outlook on life, especially his views on children. Pound warns the pregnant Hadley against trying to tame and confine Ernest: *"Mark my words. This baby will change everything. They always do. Just bear that in mind and be very careful."* (p.150)

Hemingway has a fairly good relationship with his first-born son, Bumby, but seemed conflicted in the beginning. How much of Hemingway's emotional detachment comes from Pound's influence and from his own family background?

F. Scott and Zelda Fitzgerald

- The Fitzgeralds' portrayal is two-fold: first, they are a couple in contrast to the Hemingways; second, Scott is a writer in contrast to Ernest. Fitzgerald holds Hemingway in much higher regard than the other way around.

- Having just published his world-renowned novel, *The Great Gatsby,* F. Scott Fitzgerald is both revered and envied by Ernest. He intentionally does not read the novel for a long time, perhaps because he is afraid of Fitzgerald's talent. Ernest's dislike for Fitzgerald's odd wife, Zelda, is more apparent. She is the polar opposite of Hadley: a free spirit who loves and lives as she chooses. Maybe it is Zelda's freedom that bothers Ernest because he likes having Hadley under his protection and control.

The real Ernest Hemingway was a very competitive individual in all aspects of his life and his loves. Was Fitzgerald a real or perceived threat to Ernest? Consider his reactions to other writers or individuals of equal stature to Hemingway.

The Murphys and the MacLeishes

- These two sets of friends should have been good for Hemingway, but in reality, they helped Hadley. Gerald Murphy was a painter who introduced Ernest and Hadley to the poet Archibald MacLeish and his wife, Ada.

- Notwithstanding his own comfortable family upbringing, Hemingway was quietly disdainful of the Murphy's economic status, but hid it well. It was Gerald Murphy who christened Hemingway "Papa." as Ernest taught Gerald how to ski. *"Show me again how to cut that turn at the bottom of the slope, Papa. That was a beauty."* (p.250) The nickname stuck forever.

Hemingway has no use for the moneyed class, yet avails himself freely of their generosity. Why was he so bitter about economic security and social class?

Chink

- Chink is Ernest's oldest and, perhaps, his only true friend. A comrade from the war, Chink was with Ernest when he was shot and he knew Agnes, Hemingway's first love. Of all the characters (real and fictional), Chink seems to have a keen understanding of and affection for Ernest that Hadley both appreciates and trusts. In turn, Chink treats

Hadley as a friend as opposed to how others see her, as a tool (or impediment) for Hemingway's writing. Hadley felt most relaxed around Chink. *"He was good for us, and we were good for him..."* (p.111)

Kate Smith

- A strong character in the beginning of the novel, Kate is Hadley's best friend and is in love with Ernest. Having been rejected by him, Kate turns her anger against Hadley's relationship with Ernest.

- She comes to their wedding, but disappears from the novel after it. Kate symbolizes poignantly how Hadley loses herself, her personal friendships, and her art in order to support and follow Ernest. (see Loss and Lost, p.27)

Kitty Cannell and Harold Loeb

- Kitty becomes Hadley's first real friend in Paris. As such, she is a threat to Ernest. In a complex and conflicted relationship with Harold Loeb, Kitty is both a strong force in Hadley's life and a confusing one. Desperately in love with Ernest, Hadley can't understand why Kitty stays with Harold, when he treats her so badly. He leaves her for a time to be with Lady Duff Twysden. It isn't for money, because Kitty has a large inheritance; neither is it for a lack of confidence.

  > *"She was also incredibly confident, with a way of moving and talking that communicated that she didn't need anyone to tell her she was beautiful or worthwhile. She knew it for herself, and that kind of self-possession unsettled Ernest."* (p.183)

- Hemingway immortalizes Harold Loeb as Robert Cohn and Kitty as Cohn's long suffering fiancée in his first novel, *The Sun Also Rises*.

It is Kitty who introduces Pauline to Hadley, thus sparking the unravelling of Hadley's relationship with Hemingway.

Aside from his friendship with Chink, Hemingway's connections are either toxic to begin with or are poisoned intentionally. Why has McLain chosen to emphasize this side of Hemingway? How does this influence our understanding of him as a great writer?

Pauline Pfeiffer

- Though Ernest's relationship and Hadley's friendship with Pauline does not enter the novel until close to the end, she is nevertheless a central character. A noted fashion expert, Pauline is greatly admired by Hadley for both her intelligence and her independence. Their friendship is cemented by Pauline's seemingly loyal ties to Hadley; Hadley assumes that Ernest will disapprove of Pauline as he does her other modern, well-dressed friends, but she is wrong.

- Pauline and Ernest spend more time together and their friendship grows. She champions his work and at the same time, pushes Hadley to fulfill her lifelong dream of being a concert pianist. It is with Pauline's guidance and confidence that Hadley finally takes the first step towards her own independence.

- Hadley is an innocent player in a sophisticated and high stakes environment. It takes a long time for Hadley's suspicions to be aroused. As they prepare to return to Schruns for the winter, Hemingway suggests, *"Why don't we ask Pauline to join us [...] it will be so much nicer for you if she's there."* Hadley is pleased. *"I'd love that. Aren't you sweet to think of me?"* (p.236)

- Pauline not only joins them, but they enter into a love triangle, with Pauline now firmly ensconced in the middle of Hadley's marriage to Ernest. The beginning of the end comes with Ernest's bewildering suggestion that the three of them leave Europe and move to Arkansas, where Pauline's parents own land. **(see Triangles, p.52)**

I could scarcely believe what I was hearing. 'You want us to live all together.'

'We're doing that now, aren't we?'

'Yes, and it's awful. It makes me sick to my stomach to know you're making love to her.' (p.281)

- At this realization, Hadley sadly concludes that she no longer wants to be married to him. At last, Hadley becomes her own person.

McLain hints that Pauline felt no guilt or remorse at driving a wedge between Ernest and Hadley. What is your perception of Pauline? Was she ever a true friend to Hadley or did she always have a hidden agenda?

FOCUS POINTS AND THEMES

Loss and Lost

Choice and Truth

Death, War, and Fear

Freedom and Paris

Alcohol

Family and Relationships

FOCUS POINTS AND THEMES

The primary themes of the novel — loss, alcohol, art, need, war, relationships, choice and personal freedom, and death — are similar to the themes prevalent in Ernest Hemingway's novels. His personal experiences and emotions always shaped his writing. McLain cleverly imitates this here. **(see Writing Style and Structure, p.41)**

Loss and Lost

- The theme of loss is heavily present throughout the novel, but is not just about losing external things and people. It is also about losing oneself. Both Hemingway and Hadley seem lost and directionless, even before they meet. Perhaps that was part of their mutual attraction. If so, maybe each thought of the other as their salvation.

  > *"Are you having regrets about getting married?" I tried to meet his eyes. "If you are, I can take it."*
  >
  > *"I don't know. I'm just so lost."* (p.68)

- Before meeting Hadley, Hemingway loses his father to suicide and, fairly or unfairly, blames his mother for his death. Wounded in the war, he falls in love with his nurse, Agnes, and hopes to marry her. This opportunity evaporates in her rejection letter. **(see Women, p.55)**

- His war memories and his wounds, which defined him, are lost in the passage of time. When Ernest takes Hadley to Schio to show her *"every part of the town that had managed to stay so fine in his memory, no matter what else had happened around it,"* this, too, was lost. The town had been rebuilt and changed and no one wanted to remember a terrible war that was now over. **(p.102)**

- Sadly, Hemingway squanders his many friendships, particularly those of Sherwood Anderson and Gertrude Stein, by making irrevocable and stubborn decisions.

- Worst of all, he loses Hadley, the best thing that had ever entered his life. In his memoir, *A Moveable Feast*, the real Hemingway tellingly confesses: *"I wish I had died before I had loved anyone but her."* But, as we know, he goes on to marry and "lose" three other wives before losing himself in the finality of his own suicide. His fourth wife outlived Ernest.

Hemingway was a fighter who never shied away from a battle or challenge. Was this pugilistic attitude a cover for his innate fears? Were his fears superficial or more indicative of a deeper psychological situation?

- Hadley loses her family, her friendship with Kate, Ernest's manuscripts, her art, herself, and Ernest. In fact, Hadley's voice, as the narrator of the novel, is symbolic of the theme of loss. In the beginning of the novel, Hadley describes her early years as an adventurous little girl, constantly imagining and dreaming. Her passion and spirit are evident. *"I was impulsive and talkative and curious about everything — far too curious for my mother's taste."* **(p.25)**

- Throughout her childhood, her curiosity is crushed by her family who both fear for her safety and want to repress these passion-filled ideas. Hadley becomes malleable, doing first what her mother wants and then later, following Ernest's wishes.

- After tragically losing her father to suicide, her mother to illness, and her sister Dorothea to injuries suffered in a fire, Hadley is a shell of the inquisitive child she once was. When she meets Ernest, he reignites her love of adventure and excitement. Their relationship is a strong one until she loses his life's work. Although Ernest says all the right things to Hadley, something serious has been altered. When she looked into his eyes, they *"were bruised looking and changed."* (p.137)

- The changes become still harder to ignore. With Hadley's unplanned pregnancy, their status as a couple without responsibilities is lost. This, compounded with the loss of his work, represents a loss of trust. Hemingway demanded unquestioning loyalty from Hadley and now there is doubt.

- Hadley's ultimate loss was her own identity, which she sublimated in deference to Ernest. She believed that to love him meant to dissolve the differences between them. (p.59) She even cut her hair as Ernest had requested. Seeing her reflection in a mirror, Hadley cried: *"It may have been dowdy and Victorian before, but my hair had been mine — me. What was I now?"* (p.82)

- In a last letter to Hadley, Hemingway writes: *"You've changed me more than you know, and will always be a part of everything I am. That's one thing I've learned from this. No one you love is ever truly lost."* (p.307)

  Is Hemingway right? How do you see their respective losses? Who was more successful at transforming loss into gain — Hadley or Hemingway? Consider the factors involved for each.

- We know that Hemingway was concerned with loss because his first novel, *The Sun Also Rises*, talks about the post-war generation as being battered, but not necessarily lost. His epigraph to the novel is taken from something that Gertrude Stein once said to him. *"All of you young people who served in the war. You are all a lost generation."* With this statement, she pointed the finger at Hemingway, F. Scott Fitzgerald, T. S. Eliot, and others, implying that they had no respect for anything and spent all their time drinking. **(see Freedom and Paris, p.33; see Hemingway and Company: The Facts, p.69)**

What did Stein intend with these words? What was lost — their future, their past, their moral compass, or something else?

Choice and Truth

> *Let's always tell each other the truth. We can choose that, can't we?* (p.47)

- Choice is a strong theme throughout the book, as it is in life. But in the case of Hadley and Hemingway, truth determines the direction of their relationship.

- For Hemingway, choice is bound up with telling the truth, but he doesn't always choose to do that. On assignment in Turkey, already angry and hurt by Hadley, he seems to relive his war trauma. When he consequently has an affair with an Armenian girl, he understands that he made the choice regardless of how he'll feel when he sees Hadley. *"Remember no one made you do anything. It's never anyone but you who does anything, and for that reason alone you shouldn't be sorry."* (p.120)

- Hadley considers Ernest's lack of moral integrity when he breaks his exclusive contract with the *Toronto Star* and files stories for the International News Service, using a pseudonym. *"He'd claimed it was worth it for the money. He'd work it out with his own con-*

science. I had a harder time with this dishonesty, because it seemed to speak of something larger. The way he was always out for himself, whatever the cost." (p.122)

- Ernest chooses to hurt the people he loves to ostensibly make himself happier. He chooses to vilify his friend/mentor, Sherwood Anderson, in *Torrents of Spring*. And he chooses to engage in a sexual and romantic relationship with Pauline, despite Hadley's pain over the affair. Hadley chooses to give up her own dreams to support Ernest and chooses to allow him to have another woman in their home, and ultimately, their bed.

Is there a difference between how men and women see truth as it applies to them? What do the men in Hadley's life say about their individual truth, when each has chosen to die by his own hand?

- Towards the end of the novel, it becomes clear that Ernest's propensity for self-destruction has destroyed his life. He has failed to be true to himself and the people he values.

  Now, there were only lies and compromises. He lied to everyone, beginning with himself, because it was war and you did what you had to do to stay upright. But he was losing control, if he ever had it. (p.276)

What is the bigger picture that Hadley sees and where does truth fit into it?

Death, War, and Fear

- Death is a strong theme in *The Paris Wife*. Be it through accident, illness or suicide, most of Hadley's immediate family, except for her sister, Fonnie, has died. Hadley's father shoots himself in the head, her sister Dorothea dies in a fire; her mother, from an illness. We know that in the future, Ernest kills himself with a gun.

- In Chapter 40, he contemplates the ways he might kill himself. Ultimately, he chooses the same method, a shot to the head, as Hadley's father.

- At any given time, many writers reflect on death. For example, Hemingway's contemporary, the eminent Dorothy Parker, wrote about the different methods of suicide, only to come to the conclusion that it was easier to continue to live. Hemingway, on the other hand, decided dying was easier.

- Death also takes the form of bullfighting, an ever present theme in Hemingway's novels and described in detail in *The Paris Wife*. Hemingway has an obsessive interest in bullfighting: the costumes, drama, blood, and killing. He participates in the running of the bulls, learns to use a cape like the famous toreadors, and is exhilarated by the action. The bullfighting energizes and excites him, and he wishes to share this love of the sport with everyone he is close to. When Hadley is noticed by a young torero, Ordóñez, Ernest's respect for her increases. He is disappointed and takes it personally when his friends aren't as keen on the bullfighting as he is. Everything for Ernest is a story and this one became *The Sun Also Rises*.

- The First World War was "the war to end all wars," but as we know from history, this did not happen. What it did do was destroy everyone's sense of hope and faith in the years ahead. Marriage, which is a symbol of the future, was pushed aside.

  > To marry was to say you believed in the future and in the past, too — that history and tradition and hope could stay knit together to hold you up. But the war had come and stolen all the fine young men and our faith, too. There was only today to throw yourself into without thinking about tomorrow, let alone forever.
  > (p.xi)

- Ernest maintained his friendship with Chink Dorman-Smith, who was with him in Schio before Ernest was wounded. Of all people,

Chink saw a side of Ernest that came from a shared experience and heart-to-heart talks in the middle of the night and war. No one else, not even Hadley, could see through Hemingway's bravado the way Chink could.

- McLain does an excellent job of including Chink at a critical point in Hadley's story because he explains that at the heart of Ernest's obsession with his war-time experience is Hemingway's strong sense of fear.

- Ernest Hemingway never stopped being at war, not with the enemy nor himself. He was vulnerable, yet strove to hide it with banter and bluster. But the real Hemingway, the one that Hadley shows us, is the one who was afraid of rejection in love and letters (the nurse Agnes, and publication), of the dark (he slept with the light on), and of nightmares (he suffered from them during and after the war).

- He was also afraid of being on his own. As a result, he *"literally never lived alone for as much as a year in his life. From the cradle to the grave he was himself never free of 'the softening influence of women...'"* (Spilka, p.145)

Are you surprised to see this vulnerable side of Ernest Hemingway? Why or why not?

Freedom and Paris

- The postwar '20s was a time of great flux and change. Women were coming into their own with the suffragette movement and making careers and lives for themselves outside of their families. Having been repressed during the war and before, people were eager to express themselves and find whatever means possible to become happy. For many, this meant freedom. Freedom in their thoughts, work, marriage, and life choices.

- Paris inspired freedom in all these areas. Cole Porter, a contemporary, coined the sentiment in his 1934 musical show *Anything Goes* and, truly, anything and everything was acceptable in the Hemingways' Paris. There were wonderful and creative people everywhere — painters, artists, musicians and dancers.

  > *We could walk into any café and feel the wonderful chaos of it, ordering Pernod or Rhum St. James until we were beautifully blurred and happy to be there together.* (p.xi)

- Paris gave Hemingway the starting point to his career. He met and befriended the people who set him on his career path — Gertrude Stein, Sherwood Anderson, Gerald Murphy, Ezra Pound, and others. It was also the point from which the Hemingways entered the fast life in Austria, Switzerland, and Spain. They lived an extraordinarily high lifestyle on very little income.

- McLain presents a picturesque and poignant view of Paris and Hadley's experience of it. It was where they were their best and their worst. After all, it defined the whole of her marriage to Ernest Hemingway. Once they went their separate ways, neither ever lived in Paris again.

  > *We called Paris the great good place, then, and it was. We invented it after all ... we made it with smoke and smart and savage conversation and we dared anyone to say it wasn't ours. Together we made everything and then we busted it apart again.* (p.308)

- Ernest loved Paris, perhaps more than Hadley did at first. He even loved it in the rain. *"He knew it all and loved to walk through it at night especially, dropping into cafés to see who was there and who wasn't."* (p.196) He immortalized this part of Paris in *The Sun Also Rises* and was immortalized, in turn, in Woody Allen's 2011 film, *Midnight in Paris.*

- In his memoir *A Moveable Feast*, Hemingway wrote that *"Paris was always worth it and you received return for whatever you brought to it. But this is how Paris was in the early days when we were poor and very happy."*

Alcohol

- Drinking is both a character and a theme in the novel. From the moment they meet, alcohol is an integral part of Hadley and Ernest's relationship. When things are bad or when things are good, they drink. As their marriage is falling apart, they agree to drink because it is something they do well together.

- In the '20s, as prohibition is at its height in the United States, absinthe is the drink of choice. Highly intoxicating and illegal in Paris, it is yet another way that Hemingway and the great artists of his time rebelled against societal rules and norms. It is what binds his circle of friends and holds together his marriage with Hadley.

- Paris offers the freedom to drink and even to walk down the street intoxicated without drawing attention. Alcohol provides escape from the heavy pain that is so obvious in the dialogue of the novel. One sad example is when Hadley decides to cancel her piano concert and knows that her marriage is truly over:

  > He got up and came back with a bottle of brandy and two glasses. 'Drink this,' he said, filling the tumbler and passing it across the table. 'You could use it.'
  > 'Yes, let's get stinking drunk.'
  > 'All right. We've always been good at that.' (p.261)

- Hadley, Hemingway, and their friends are always drinking. It's difficult to assess whether they were influenced by their times or the times were influenced by them. The Great War was over and the Depression had not yet occurred. Prohibition would be a failure and

the social constraints of the day (love and marriage) were upended. Hemingway reflected much of this in *The Sun Also Rises.*

> *[The] Hemingway of the middle twenties ... expressed the romantic disillusion and set the favorite pose for the period. It was the moment of gallantry in heartbreak, grim and nonchalant banter, and heroic dissipation. The great watchword was 'Have a drink'; and in the bars of New York and Paris the young people were getting to talk like Hemingway.* (Wilson, p.75)

Hadley seems very comfortable with the role alcohol played in their lives, but it does not define her the way it does Hemingway. How do they differ from each other when it comes to drink?

Family and Relationships

- Relationships, friendships, marriage, and love affairs are central to the novel and they have everything to do with family — both Hemingway's and Hadley's. They are fraught with tension, envy, admiration, pain, loss, love, betrayal, and suffering.

- Both Ernest and Hadley are innocent and inexperienced. Ernest was 18 when he went to war and was wounded. As often happens, he fell in love with his nurse, Agnes. He was always a charmer and he believed she fell in love with him. Agnes was older and probably did care for Ernest. She rejected his marriage proposal in a letter which devastated Ernest for years to come. **(see Agnes von Kurowsky, p.70)**

In an interesting parallel, Hemingway proposed to Hadley in a letter, as McLain writes on p.50. Consider the implications of these impersonal approaches to the very emotional subject of marriage. Why is Hemingway so cavalier towards Hadley when he is still so angry with Agnes?

- Hadley's only romantic interest before Ernest was an unrequited crush on her piano teacher. *"I could listen to him talk about anything, and I suppose that's how it started, with admiration and envy."* (p.18) This is also how she feels about Ernest Hemingway.

- Perhaps because she lost her father at a young age or because she sees her mother as cold and untouchable, Hadley's relationships with men revolve around power. Hadley has none; Ernest has it all. She gives herself over totally, falling for those whose art consumes them.

- Hadley also gives up her American friends when she heads to Paris. Although she makes new ones, they are always connected to Ernest. With Kate no longer in the picture, Hadley is friends with Kitty, but Ernest tries to sabotage that relationship. The only woman he encourages as a friend to Hadley is Pauline, but that has its own sad and poignant outcome.

- Hadley and Ernest had similar family backgrounds. Both had domineering mothers whom they resented. Hadley blamed her mother for the death of her father. He was an alcoholic. Their relationship was difficult and distant. When her mother died, Hadley was able to let herself fall under the magnetic spell of Ernest's strong personality. Despite her age (29), Hadley had not yet decided who she would become.

Hadley perceived her life with Ernest to be free of the pressures that her mother wanted to impose on her. Was she right or did she overlook the fact that she was still being told what to do, how to look, and how to behave?

- Ernest resented his family from the time he was a child. He could never bear his mother and resented her relationship with the father he adored. In his letters to Hadley, he referred to his mother as a "bitch." His extreme anger unsettled Hadley because she recognized his emotions in herself. (p.39) **(see The Sun Also Rises, p.72)**

- The most telling part of Hemingway's response to family was his continual struggle for their approval. He sent them a copy of his first published book, *Three Stories and Ten Poems*. Instead of praise, Ernest got a letter of condemnation from his father.

  > *"To hell with them anyway," he said, but he kept the letter, folding it carefully and putting it in the dresser where he stored all of his important correspondence.* Families can be vicious, *he was fond of saying* ... (p.193)

- Hadley had once asked Ernest if he was attracted to her because of the similarity of their mothers. She also knew that Ernest had the same qualities and tendencies toward alcoholism and depression that her father did.

  How much did the influence of their family backgrounds have on their feelings for each other? How common is this in other couples?

WRITING STYLE AND STRUCTURE

Title

Setting

Narration

Epigraphs

Italics

Iceberg Theory

Repetition

WRITING STYLE AND STRUCTURE

Title

- The title *The Paris Wife* tells it all. It implies that there is more than one wife, and that Paris is the focal point of Hadley and Ernest's marriage. It is where he eventually finds success and where their marriage falls apart. It is where Hadley both loses and finds herself. **(see Loss and Lost, p.27)**

Setting

- The setting of the novel is equally important. From Paris to Spain, Toronto to Switzerland and Germany, Hadley follows Ernest around the world. But it is Paris that is the center of their relationship. *"There is no cure for Paris,"* she says on the very first page of the novel.

- Sherwood Anderson convinced Hemingway to go to Paris because it was where the inspiration for modern writing could be found and

where Hemingway could make important contacts. *"Paris was where a young man could make it as a writer."* (Jones, p.7) It was the intoxicating epicenter for expatriate philosophers, writers, artists, and radical thinkers. Ideas and inspiration filled the air. **(see Freedom and Paris, p.33)**

- The Hemingways lived mostly on Hadley's inheritance from an uncle and on the little that Ernest brought in from his journalism. And yet, they lived the same decadent life that Hemingway describes so crisply in *The Sun Also Rises.* Traveling around Europe, they socialized, drank, skied, drank, attended bullfights, drank, fished, and drank some more. No one seemed to work for weeks and months on end. Money and alcohol were readily available.

- The only period of their marriage that was unromantic was when they chose to go to Toronto, where Hadley would give birth to their son and Ernest would work for the *Toronto Star.* Ernest hated his job and the managing editor, Harry Hindmarsh, hated him. The situation was so bad that Ernest missed Bumby's birth because Hindmarsh wouldn't give him the time off.

- A crying baby, silly assignments, and no time for Ernest's own writing convinced Hadley that they had to return to Paris. She traded the welfare of her child for the welfare of her husband. **(see Choice and Truth, p.30)**

> *Some men would have been able to choke it back and take it for a while, but he might have lost himself completely there. Ahead in Paris, it was anyone's guess how we'd make it, but I couldn't worry about that. Ernest needed me to be strong for us both now, and I would be ... I was choosing him, the writer, in Paris.* (p.173)

Narration

- The narration of the novel is done entirely in Hadley's voice. A first person technique allows the reader to feel a part of the story and to identify with the narrator.

- Hadley speaks in a way that sometimes mimics how Hemingway wrote — short, declarative sentences with no extraneous descriptions or information. This was Gertrude Stein's advice to him and is the successful narrative structure of his first Paris novel, *The Sun Also Rises*. (see Hemingway and Company: The Facts, p.69)

- Whether this is an homage to Hemingway or a technique to exemplify how completely Hadley wrapped herself in Ernest remains a question. However, McLain does an excellent job of depicting Hadley's evolution from a lost little girl to a wife and mother overcome by her husband's passion and self-destructiveness. Hadley fades into herself and the life Ernest has created. They look alike, talk alike and even have the same nickname for each other — Tatie. Hadley transforms herself so completely, we are not sure what her true voice is until their marriage falters and fails.

What is your perception of Hadley's voice and persona? Does she present herself as an individual or an extension of her husband?

If you are familiar with Hemingway's work, compare and contrast it with McLain's narrative structure and style. If not, consider how successfully McLain has created Hadley as a narrator.

Epigraphs

- McLain cleverly quotes Gertrude Stein and Ernest Hemingway himself in the epigraphs which identify the key thoughts of the novel. Stein once said, *"It is not what France gave you but what it did not take from you that was important."* She was talking about her own life in Paris, but these words directly apply to Hadley. When Hadley's marriage dissolved, she could have dissolved with it. Instead, she went back to the States temporarily.

> *Bumby and I returned to Paris after our summer in Carmel. He missed his father terribly and, honestly, I didn't know where else I should go.* (p.310)

Hadley met Paul Mowrer, a journalist colleague of Ernest's, and married him. Paul was solid and stable, just what Hadley needed at that point.

What things did Paris take from Hadley Richardson, and what did it give to her? Paris had the potential to destroy her, but perhaps, the city made her stronger. Do you agree or disagree?

- The second epigraph quotes Hemingway: *"There's no one thing that's true. It's all true."* As far as fiction is concerned, there are shades, variations, and different meanings of the word "true." His romantic goal for himself and Hadley was to always tell each other the truth. His literary goal was to *"write one true sentence ... simple and true, every day ..."* (p.81) He wanted his characters to be *"just like us, just people trying to live simply and say what they really mean."* (p.58) **(see Choice and Truth, p.30)**

Ernest Hemingway hoped to blend his life and art into one and, as a result, he created his own mythology. **(see Ernest Heminway: Man, Myth, Impact, p.67)**

How does using the word "true," meaning honest, apply or not apply to Hemingway? Does the word "true," meaning genuine, fit Hemingway as the person or the character he created?

Italics

- McLain copies a common Hemingway technique with her five italicized passages. The first time he used this format was in his short story "The Snows of Kilimanjaro," where the character's interior monologues were meant to juxtapose memory (past) and regret (present).

    o Ch. 9 of *The Paris Wife* has Hemingway reflecting on his treatment of Kate. He was about to marry Hadley, but recalls how, just the year before, Kate terrified him with her flaunted sexuality.

    o Ch. 18 finds Hemingway in Turkey on assignment. He cheats on Hadley not once, but twice, with the same woman. He considers it a residual part of his war wounds.

    o In Ch. 37, Hemingway is entranced by Pauline and wonders why he can't have both her and Hadley.

    o In Ch. 40, Hemingway realizes that the different parts of himself are battling it out for his sanity and his very life. He considers different methods of suicide if there is no resolution.

    o Ch. 45 places Ernest at the end of his marriage to Hadley. He considers Hadley his past and Pauline his future.

- Many writers now use this technique to visually separate various thought processes in a novel. Hemingway used it to portray a character's state of emotion and to place that emotion in-between the character's past and present motivations. McLain uses it so that the reader can get into Hemingway's head without pushing Hadley aside.

Does knowing Hemingway's inner thoughts enhance Hadley's story or detract from it?

Iceberg Theory

- Ezra Pound and Gertrude Stein were Hemingway's most profound writing influences. Stein encouraged him to be *"simple and quite clear"* and not to pose or embellish his ideas. (p.88) Pound said much of the same thing. *"Cut everything superfluous ... Go in fear of abstractions. Don't tell readers what to think. Let the action speak for itself."* (p.89) Consequently, Hemingway pioneered a theory of omission. The reader is made to work to retrieve the story's submerged meaning. Hemingway's writing illuminated the words, but didn't explain them.

- This led directly to Hemingway's iceberg theory, which he explains in his non-fiction book about bullfighting, *Death in the Afternoon.*

  If a writer of prose knows enough of what he is writing about he may omit things that he knows and the reader, if the writer is writing truly enough, will have a feeling of those things as strongly as though the writer had stated them. The dignity of movement of an ice-berg is due to only one-eighth of it being above water. A writer who omits things because he does not know them only makes hollow places in his writing.

- Thankfully, McLain does not leave the reader to guess important details about Hadley's life, precisely because Hadley is an open book, unlike her husband. But there are clues about the development of Hemingway's writing that are embedded throughout Hadley's narration. They help to explain Hemingway's trial and error efforts to produce his first novel, *The Sun Also Rises.* (see The Sun Also Rises, p.72)

Repetition

- Readers who are unfamiliar with Hemingway may not realize the deliberate nature of repetition in his work. Words and phrases are restated often and dialogue is reduced to a continuous stream of *"he said, she said."* Hemingway wanted to bring the speakers words forward in a realistic and straightforward way without distracting the reader with descriptive side comments. He wanted his characters to reveal more things about themselves than they realized. **(see Iceberg Theory, p.46)** In some of Hemingway's novels and stories, the dialogue never discloses the topic under discussion, but talks around it.

- There may be two sources for this technique. First, Hemingway was a journalist, used to setting down repeated details for the sake of clarity and precision. Secondly, Gertrude Stein had a large influence on his style. She would repeatedly name simple objects over and over, without varying the word, *"reveling in how any word took on a striking power when you used it again and again."* **(p.107)** Hadley tells us the effect this had on Hemingway's writing and how he was able to use it to bring hidden concepts to the forefront of the reader's awareness.

  > *In some of the new Nick Adams passages, I saw how he was doing this, too, with the simplest language and things — lake, trout, log, boat — and how it gave the work a very distilled and almost mythic feel.* **(p.107)**

- Although McLain claims to have not used Hemingway's techniques in her writing, there are descriptions of people and incidents that can be traced back to his style. Her sentences, descriptions, and conversations are fairly short, clear, and to the point.

- McLain makes the point that Hemingway and Hadley had an intimate way of speaking to each other that probably influenced Hemingway's story-telling techniques. As for herself, McLain said in an interview with Bookclub-in-a-Box that she feels she read so much by and about Hemingway that his style may have entered her own writing subconsciously by "osmosis." **(see In Her Own Words, p.59)**

- Perhaps one of the things McLain repeats most often is the foreshadowing of the end of Hadley's marriage to Ernest.

Notice how McLain uses dialogue. What other repetitions do you notice? Taking into account McLain's style and Hemingway's style of writing, do you see similarities or differences?

SYMBOLS

Boxing and Bullfighting

Triangles

Suicide

Women

SYMBOLS

It's hard to say that the following are symbols in the usual literary sense, but they are so close to encapsulating Hemingway's personality and persona that they become metaphors for him and his relationship with both the world and Hadley. McLain places Hadley at the edges of these symbols, as an observer and a mirror.

Boxing and Bullfighting

- Whether it's boxing (man vs. man) or bullfighting (man vs. animal), it is all about competition and bravado. Ernest would fight anyone for fun, but from the beginning Hadley sees that for Ernest, the fight was for competition. *"... the match went on good-naturedly, but I'd seen the killer look on Ernest's face when he threw the punch and knew it was all very serious to him. He wanted to win."* (p.12)

- Both boxing and bullfighting can be placed in a war-like arena, where there is every danger of being injured or killed. Each represents virile masculinity. The first depends on the brute strength of the human fighter; the second exemplifies the brute strength of the animal. Hemingway, the writer, makes a great show of his potency and vigor.

- The main character, Jake, in *The Sun Also Rises* becomes impotent through a war wound. The entire Paris contingent of friends that the Hemingways hang out with are aimless and unfulfilled. (see **Loss and Lost, p.27**) The purpose of their lives has been mortally wounded. The side of Hemingway that Hadley exposes is the vulnerable, small boy, confined inside the man.

- Bullfighting is similar to boxing because the bull is deliberately cornered by the bullfighter. Because Hemingway was such a good writer, he drafted a story about bullfighting before ever seeing one firsthand. He and Hadley joined Bob McAlmon, a friend of Ezra Pound's. Bob had started a new company, Contact Editions, which Ernest hoped would publish him.

- Ernest loved the atmosphere of the bullfight from the very first time he set foot in Pamplona. He and Hadley were with Bill, Harold, and Duff. At the end of the first fight, no one was more surprised than Hemingway when the matador, Ordóñez sliced off the bull's ear and handed it to Hadley as an honor. (p.220-226)

- The Hemingways' whole first experience in Pamplona is set out in detail in Ernest's novel *The Sun Also Rises*.

The interesting thing is that Hadley was never mentioned in the novel, and she was quite hurt by the omission. At the time, Hadley and Ernest were still happy and she was expecting their child, Bumby. Why would Hemingway have deliberately not included Hadley in this book? Were the signs of trouble already present?

Triangles

- McLain focuses much of her attention on the idea of triangles and where, in the configuration, Hadley finds herself. The first "lopsided triangle" Hadley is a part of is with Ernest and Kate. (p.44) She had to choose and she chose Ernest.

- Hadley finds herself surrounded by other triangular configurations: Gertrude Stein and Ernest, Jinny and Pauline, Kitty and Ernest. The Paris that Hadley knew was filled with *"every combination of sexual pairing and triangulation."* (p.154)

- By the time Pauline and Ernest were in the middle of their affair, the triangle was set in stone.

> *At our hotel, there were three of everything — three breakfast trays, three terry-cloth robes, three wet bathing suits on the line. On the crushed rock path ... three bicycles stood on their stands. If you looked at the bicycles one way, they looked very solid ... if you looked at them another way, you could see just how thin each kickstand was under the weight of the heavy frame, and how they were poised to fall like dominoes or the skeletons of elephants or like love itself. But when I noticed this, I kept it to myself because that, too, was part of the unwritten contract.* (p.283)

The important part of the bargain was to keep on drinking and to stay quiet.

Why did Hadley buy into this unspoken pact? She was the wife and had legal and moral rights. What kept her from reacting to this for such a long time?

Suicide

- It is a well-known fact that Ernest Hemingway died by his own hand in 1961. Suicide and self-destruction were part of a path that Hemingway set himself on during and after the war. Paula McLain makes it one of the first points of the book.

> *There was no back home anymore, not in the essential way, and that was part of Paris, too. Why we couldn't*

stop drinking or talking or kissing the wrong people no matter what it ruined. Some of us had looked into the faces of the dead and tried not to remember anything in particular. Ernest was one of these. (Prologue, ix)

- Hemingway becomes increasingly cantankerous with the people in his life, especially people like Sherwood Anderson and Gertrude Stein, who helped to build his career and his image. He stampedes haphazardly over friendships and connections the way a frightened bull does during the running of the bulls. (see **Boxing and Bullfighting, p.51**)

   I knew Ernest's bravado was almost entirely invented, but I hated to think of all the good friends we'd lost because of his pride and volatile temper ... (p.269)

- Hadley had already suffered through the suicide of her own father and was sensitive to Ernest's dark moods. She had seen glimmers of his sagging emotions, but hadn't observed a full-blown turning point until just before their wedding. She wondered whether he was having second thoughts. His response was that he felt lost.

   What did it all mean? Was this crisis related to his experiences in the war? ... or was this more personal? Did this sadness belong to Ernest in the fatal way my father's belonged to him? (p.69)

- Ernest Hemingway took his life in the exact manner that Hadley's father had taken his. *"Maybe it wasn't irony at all, but the purest and saddest sort of history."* (p.313) Hadley's father, Ernest's father, and Ernest's brother all shot and killed themselves. In the end, Hadley wasn't surprised. *"Death was always there for him, sometimes only barely balanced out."* (p.313)

What was the possible connection between Hadley's love for Ernest and her love for her father? In choosing Ernest, did Hadley choose her father?

How common is it for children of suicides to become attracted to others suffering similar psychological pain? Was there anything Hadley could have done differently?

Was McLain's portrayal of this painful part of the Hemingways' story successful? If yes, what made it so? If not, why not?

Women

- For all of his adult life, Hemingway was not without a wife or a lover. However, in his writing, he includes women more often than not as accessories to strong male characters or as sexual images against which a man's virile nature can be juxtaposed.

- In *The Paris Wife*, Hadley becomes very aware of this when she feels jealous of Hemingway's attentions to Duff. When she eventually sees the actual pages of *The Sun Also Rises*, Hadley understands that *"Ernest was a writer, not Duff's lover. He'd seen her as a character, maybe even from the beginning. And now that he was living in the book ... the tension and ugliness (of Pamplona) could be useful."* (p.226)

- Another potent question concerns Hadley and her sense of womanhood. In this early part of the century, women were coming into their own. The 21st century's new woman was strong, daring, free-thinking, sexually promiscuous and could fit well into the easy way of life in Paris.

- Hadley's mother and sister, Fonnie, had been active members of the Suffragette movement. Hadley was at odds with them and with the women she observed at Kenley's parties in Chicago. Compared to these very modern girls, Hadley was *"closer to a Victorian holdout than a flapper."* (p.7)

What did Hemingway see in her? Why was he so instantly attracted?

What are your impressions of Hemingway and his women?

While all the women in *The Paris Wife* are real historical personalities, did McLain capture the variations of Hemingway's needs, hopes, and perspectives as far as these women were concerned?

Did McLain effectively capture Hadley's needs, hopes, and perspectives in juxtaposition to Hemingway and his view of women?

IN HER OWN WORDS:
Q&A WITH PAULA MCLAIN

IN HER OWN WORDS
Paula McLain, October 2011

Countless memoirs and biographies have been written about the great artists who lived in Paris during the 1920s, a time that Woody Allen refers to as the "literary Golden Age" in his 2011 film *Midnight in Paris*. But long before that interpretation hit screens, Paula McLain was inspired by Ernest Hemingway's work, and McLain hit the books to gain a better understanding of the (ultimately doomed) relationship between Hadley and Ernest. McLain spoke to Bookclub-in-a-Box from her home in Chicago about her novel *The Paris Wife*.

Bookclub-in-a-Box: The *New York Times* book review for *The Paris Wife* says that Hadley was "a very fine and decent person, but she was the starter wife of a man who wound up treating her terribly. Had she not married him, no novelist would be telling her story." What was it about Hadley that made you want to build a novel around her as a protagonist, instead of writing about Hemingway himself?

Paula McLain: Well, because I disagree with that reviewer. I must, in order to spend so much time committed to this book and this story, and her as a character. I do disagree. I actually think she has a really worthwhile point of view. I think "starter wife" is so insulting, because in order to write the book and devote myself to unraveling their love story, I have to believe that

their connection was profound, and that they understood something pretty significant about one another, and that their love story was moving and transcended their own weaknesses and time. If you read *A Moveable Feast*, you see his regret, and not just guilt, but that he believed somewhere along the way he lost a version of himself that really was a better man than he ended up being. And some of that had to do with the love he had with Hadley and his friendship and connection with her.

So my inspiration was reading *A Moveable Feast* and wondering who these young people were and how they found one another. What I found convinced me that the rise and fall of their marriage was a story worth telling. She is this woman who's not ambitious as an artist, and isn't hungry the same way that he is. That was an interesting point of view to me, that she would be looking in on all of this from her perspective as a woman and a mother and a muse and a friend and a lover, and all of those much quieter sorts of vantage points.

There's a lot in *The Paris Wife* about how Hadley had trouble coping with the bohemian artists' lifestyle, and the way that Hemingway flirted with other women. Hadley even says in your book, "his preoccupation with his work made me sharply aware that I had no passion of my own." Was it frustrating for you that Ernest always seemed to be the center of her universe, and that she didn't have very much ambition of her own?

It was, because she was very much unlike me as a woman. My creative life is the most important thing in the world to me, even though I'm also a mother. I wouldn't want to part with that, ever, and I think she saw that in Hemingway and wished she had an all-consuming passion for her own art — everybody said that she was a wonderful pianist, but I think it was her nerves. She never got over stage fright, or maybe she didn't have a creative personality, but she never made that leap to make that the central point in her universe, and she saw that he did have that. I think she was jealous, in a way, of the way his work fit in.

So sometimes, yes, I wanted to pick her up and shake her, but ultimately, the more time I spent with her, I believe that I wanted to take her on her own terms, in that context in her day and age. And I believe that she was a

woman between generations. Even though she saw these modern women around her, she wasn't that. But she also wasn't her own mother, or her own sister, who kind of were controlling and domineering and selfish. Her partnership with Ernest — and I believe it was really a partnership — some women look at it and say, "Oh, she's consumed herself with his career and his ego," but I believe in a way, for a short time, she did get exactly what she wanted. She wanted to have this life with this person making brilliant work and she got that. I think that's hard for us to understand in our generation of women, how she could subsume herself and still get what she wanted.

[…] What she said at the end of her life was that he gave her the keys to the world, and that meeting him, she explored another life. If you look at her trajectory, this very quiet, Victorian girl who was sheltered to the degree that she almost had no life at all, she became super strong, and her physical endurance, her resilience, her zest for life increased tenfold when she met Ernest Hemingway. And I think you have to hold on to that: they did in their early days enjoy their lives, each other, and what life had to offer. Even though they lost each other in the end, it's pretty profound that at the end of their lives, they still loved and admired and respected each other.

There are parts in the book where you're writing from Hadley's perspective but it still seems reminiscent of Hemingway's writing style. Did you write in his style as homage to him, or were you trying to convey how much of Ernest was in Hadley's voice?

I think I was trying to convey how much they became part of one another's lives, and also, with the speech rhythms, I think they each were influenced by the other. So when he says something like, "With you by my side, I think I can write a novel, I think I can do anything at all. I want to start with real people just talking to each other and saying what they really mean," I think, in his mind, that's just him and Hadley, talking. So when you read his early stories from *In Our Time*, I think the dialogue sounds very much like her letters.

And also, I think I would have been terrified if that had been my objective. Oh my god — to deliberately set out and write in Hemingway-esque prose.

But I think some of it did happen by osmosis, because I was reading so much Hemingway and his correspondence, so it was like it was in my bloodstream.

Have you visited Paris since you wrote this book?

I have. I couldn't go to Paris when I was drafting the first chunk because I was dead broke. I had quit my teaching job, and I didn't really have money to go around the corner. But when the book sold, my way of celebrating was to go on what I called my "Stalking Hemingway Tour of France and Spain." So I went to Paris and Pamplona. If you've been to Paris, you'll see that everything still stands. You can stand in front of their first apartment at Cardinal Lesmoines, and there's where Hemingway used to write, and there's where the Fitzgeralds used to live, and Ezra Pound's studio. It's incredible to feel that physically connected to their experiences. I try to picture myself in those places and I feel like I was there.

Are you working on another book now?

I'm contracted to write another historical novel about another actual, living person. But this is not a woman-behind-the-man story — I'm writing a novel about Marie Curie. I think she's totally fascinating and I'm really enjoying my research and trying to get close to her vantage point. Surprisingly, she's a very passionate person, and she's got great love stories and personal tragedy. I'm actually smiling while I say that, "personal tragedy," and yet that's my sweet spot as a novelist; I need to feel like there's something emotionally dramatic at stake for my character. The science is terrifying for me, I'm waiting to see if there's a book out there called *Radion for Dummies*.

I like this genre, but I'm sure I'll be lambasted. I've read other pieces saying, 'What is this, literary body-snatching?' Nobody quite knows what to call it — fictional autobiography? But I love the fact that I can just completely disappear into history, into the mind and heart of a character who is part invention and part based on fact, and I'm getting a history lesson but I'm falling through this wonderful trap door into another time and place.

It's completely captivating for me as a novelist, and I just love every second of it. So why not just do what we like to do, instead of second-guessing yourself or thinking about what the market will bear, or what critics will say? I'm having a good time.

Have you seen the 2011 Woody Allen movie, *Midnight in Paris*, based on the same time and place?

I have! It was so funny to me, because I started getting emails from friends and fans saying, "Have you seen this new movie? Hemingway is in it!" And I thought, how could that be? Because I didn't even hear any buzz for this film, it just appeared this summer, and I have to say that I owe Mr. Allen a big thank you, because he boosted my sales. It was perfect timing. Readers were then going on to watch the movie, or people who had watched the movie would be asked, "Have you read this book?" They just kind of bounced off each other that way, and I got on a lot of summer reading lists, I think, because of that movie and the current appetite for the Jazz Age. It's really interesting to me, the way trends run, and that he and I were thinking about that at the same time.

What are you reading now — not for research, but for pleasure?

I just finished Jeffrey Eugenides' new book, *The Marriage Plot*. I'm reviewing it for the *Washington Independent Review of Books*, which is why I got an early copy, and it's so good! At first I thought, this can't be a Jeffrey Eugenides novel, because it's so quiet. It's about these three characters in the summer, the year after they graduate from Brown in 1983, and it's just about love relationships, but the breadth and depth of this novel is really surprising. I loved it, and I was really taken in by it.

Which books were key to Paula McLain's research of Ernest Hemingway and Hadley Richardson?

- *Ernest Hemingway: A Life Story,* by Carlos Baker (1969)
Paula says: "This is what I used for my main framework."

- *Hadley: The First Mrs. Hemingway,* by Alice Hunt Sokoloff (1973)
Paula says: "Alice was Hadley's friend and duet partner, and because Hadley was still alive, I think she was afraid to expose her in any way. So it's really warm and generous to Hadley, but not a great place to get information. You get a real feel for her as a person, even though you don't get a lot of dirt."

- *Hadley,* by Gioia Diliberto (1992)
Paula says: "It's actually really very rich, and that was super useful to me."

- *The Hemingway Women,* by Bernice Kert (1983)
Paula says: "It's wonderful. It runs the whole gamut from Hemingway's mother Grace to Agnes von Kurowsky [the nurse he fell in love with after the war] to all his wives and lovers, and that's fascinating to read."

- *The True Gen,* by Denis Brian (1988)
Paula says: "The author takes all these big questions, like Hadley losing the valise, or Hemingway's war wounds, or points of contention, and he just asks everyone who knew the man to weigh in, including friends, editors, wives, lovers, psychologists, and biographers."

LAST THOUGHTS

Ernest Hemingway: Man, Myth, Impact

Hemingway and Company: The Facts

The Sun Also Rises

Suggested Beginnings

LAST THOUGHTS

Ernest Hemingway: Man, Myth, Impact

- So much has been written about Hemingway by others, but much of what they have written was put into place by the man himself. He was a physically imposing man and was never satisfied with merely being excellent at writing, fishing, and boxing.

> *He had to turn himself into a Homeric myth, which meant posing and lying, treating life as fiction ... We know Hemingway the man not from letters and diaries but from tales told by himself in bars, on shipboard, on safari, tales in their turn retailed by others, reminiscences which truckle to the legend and are ... growing all the time less reliable as their subject recedes into history.* (Burgess)

- Decades after his death, the stories are still coming in. Literary critic Harold Bloom claims that *"more people have a recognition of the Hemingway myth than have ever read Hemingway. He lives on in the public imagination as Papa, the hard-drinking big-game hunter, war correspondent and pugilist ... We associate him with Paris of the 1920s, Madrid in the 1930s and after that a blend of Havana and Key West, until he went home to emulate his father's suicide."* (Bloom)

- McLain's extraordinary accomplishment is that she gives us another version of the man behind the Man. Using Hadley's voice and memories, McLain draws a new outline — a very human Ernest Hemingway who struggled with living and loving, while on his way to becoming something special.

> *After he left for the States, I saw him just twice more ..., but I watched from a distance as he became, very quickly, the most important writer of his generation and also a kind of hero of his own making ... The myth he was creating out of his own life was big enough ... but under this, I knew he was still lost. That he slept with the light on or couldn't sleep at all, that he feared death so much he sought it out wherever and however he could. He was such an enigma, really — fine and strong and weak and cruel. An incomparable friend and a son of a bitch. In the end, there wasn't one thing about him that was truer than the rest. It was all true.*
> (p.311) **(see Choice and Truth, p.30)**

- Hemingway's impact on modern literature is immeasurable. He gave the world new literary models to follow – a different shape of character hero (both male and female), dialogue as the main form of plot advancement, the use of a small number of symbols to suggest a greater number of different abstract ideas, and a few well-placed descriptive paragraphs that set off the dialogues that fall on either side of them.

- His reputation sits comfortably alongside the other greats of his era – James Joyce, Ezra Pound, and F. Scott Fitzgerald, all of whom we meet in McLain's pages. But it was Hemingway, above all, who transferred the mantle of literature from the writer to the reader.

- In the literary world, Ernest Hemingway is something of an anomaly. His contemporaries praised him. Critics enjoy his work as well, as is evidenced by his Pulitzer Prize and Nobel laureateship. Yet his novels are not widely read, despite their immense value.

Hemingway's fiction demands multiple readings and careful consideration — a tall order given the frenetic pace of modern life. But those who put in the effort to do so are invariably rewarded.

If Hemingway (and others like him) are so difficult to read and access, why should we bother? What does the understanding of a writer like Hemingway give to modern readers?

Does Paula McLain add to that understanding? If so, how?

Hemingway and Company: The Facts

Ernest Hemingway

- Hemingway was born in Oak Park, Illinois on July 21, 1899 and died in Ketchum, Idaho on July 2, 1961.

- In 1918, Hemingway was part of the Red Cross Ambulance Corps in Italy. He was wounded on July 8. Before he became established as a novelist, he was a journalist for the *Toronto Star* newspaper, both locally and internationally.

- He was awarded the Pulitzer Prize (1952) and the Nobel prize in literature (1954). Many of his books have been made into films.

- There were four Hemingway wives:

  o Elizabeth Hadley Richardson (1921–1927; divorced)
  o Pauline Pfeiffer (1927–1940; divorced)
  o Martha Gellhorn (1940–1945; divorced)
  o Mary Welsh Hemingway (1946–1961; widow)

- Hemingway had three sons: John "Bumby" Hadley Nicanor Hemingway, named for a famous matador, born to Hadley, and Patrick and Gregory, born to Pauline. At this point in time, only Patrick is living.

- John (also known as Jack, or Bumby) was born in Toronto, Canada. His godparents were Gertrude Stein and Alice B. Toklas, and he was later the father of Margaux and Mariel Hemingway. Margaux was another Hemingway who took her own life. John died in 2000 as a result of surgical complications.

- Gregory's son, also named John, is a Montreal-based writer who has written his own memoir of the family, called *Strange Tribe: A Family Memoir*. He did not know his grandfather, Ernest, but recounts the story through his father's eyes.

  The mythic image of my grandfather is a powerful one — the macho avenger. The hunter, the fisherman, the war hero, the conqueror of women, married four times, plenty of affairs — in fact, he was far more complicated than that ... He was a far more fragile person than people think. He was also interested in the entire spectrum of human sexuality, about the intersection that could happen between men and women. (Hays)

The Hemingway family seems to have been particularly prone to depression and suicide. Currently, there is much more open and accessible information on these conditions. Consider whether treatment and intervention would have helped Ernest. Given his characterization, would he have been open to it?

Agnes von Kurowsky

- Agnes was the American nurse who looked after Hemingway when he was wounded in Italy. Like Hadley, Agnes was older than Ernest (by seven years). He fell deeply in love with her and promised to marry her. When he returned to the States, a letter from Agnes followed in which she rejected his marriage proposal.

- Whether she was truly in love with Ernest or saw him as a lovely and charming adolescent is one of the mysteries of the Hemingway myth. But there is no doubt that Agnes had a profound effect on his life and his work.

- McLain brings it up as an important emotional exchange between Ernest and Hadley. Hadley observes that his love for Agnes was not a *"new story ... (but) it was the only story for him."* (p.45) Hadley realizes that Ernest was not only affected by losing Agnes, but more so by the fact that he believed she lied to him. She and Ernest pledge to always tell each other the truth. (p.47)

- Hemingway deals with Agnes' story in his novel *A Farewell to Arms*.

Hadley Richardson

- Hadley was born in St. Louis on Nov. 9, 1891, and died Jan. 22, 1979. Hadley met and married Ernest Hemingway in the span of a year, just months after her mother's death. They were married for five years, the majority of which was spent in Paris. Hadley married Paul Mowrer, a journalist, in 1933.

- How exciting it must have been in Paris in the 1920s. Although many of Hemingway's compatriots were already making their name in artistic and literary circles, they had not yet become the icons they are today. Hadley introduces us to Gertrude Stein, Alice B. Toklas, Ezra Pound and his wife, Scott and Zelda Fitzgerald, Sherwood Anderson, and a host of other notable members of the time, as she must have seen them.

- Many biographical treatments of the era and its participants contain details and statistics. McLain has treated us to an inside and up-close look at the personalities behind the artistic celebrities of the last century.

The Sun Also Rises

- *The Sun Also Rises* was Ernest Hemingway's first novel, published in 1926. The first of two epigraphs in *The Paris Wife* is the famous quote from Gertrude Stein: *"You are all a lost generation."* (see **Loss and Lost, p.27**) Stein's words, which form the epigraph to *The Sun Also Rises*, define both novels, as a reflection of the psychological and emotional devastation caused by the First World War. The vets who survived returned home desensitized to violence and war, disillusioned and without a sense of purpose. They had lost their adolescence and early adulthood. They felt that another war would not have the same effect on this generation, given all they had seen and suffered.

- Hemingway's novel dwells on social relationships, masculinity, impotence, and escapism (alcohol and travel). The main character, Jake, ponders how to get the most out of life and wonders if hard work for the future is an answer or if it is living and spending in the now.

- The characters in *The Sun Also Rises* are the very people that Hadley and Ernest hung around with in Paris and Spain. Life in the novel is in many ways a mirror image of life as the Hemingways lived it. In the novel's early drafts, Hemingway even referred to the main character, Jake, as "Hem." Like Hemingway, Jake was a journalist living in Paris, had volunteered as an ambulance driver during the war, was wounded, and also had a passion for bullfighting. The other characters were based on Lady Duff Twysden, Harold Loeb, and the real bullfighter, Cayetano Ordóñez. Missing are Hadley (whom Ernest left out deliberately) and Pauline (with whom his relationship had not yet blossomed).

- This was Hemingway's first published novel and it was exceedingly well received in Europe, but not so well, at first, in North America. The stumbling block turned out to be Hemingway's penchant for profanity. He wanted to use certain words which he felt would help set up the book's atmosphere. All the negative and profane words were removed, but Hemingway insisted on keeping the word "bitch." In a letter to his editor, Max Perkins, Hemingway wrote:

> *... in the matter of the use of the Bitch by Brett – I have never once used this word ornamentally nor except when it was absolutely necessary and I believe the few places where it is used must stand ...* (O'Donnell)

- This novel, along with 65 others, was banned in Boston in 1926. With it, Hemingway joined the also-banned company of James Joyce, D.H. Lawrence, and more. *A Farewell to Arms* and *For Whom the Bell Tolls* were banned in other places at a later time.

Consider the notion of censorship and book-banning and where these ideas relate to cutting-edge art and literature. Have things changed?

The Sun Also Rises was written nearly 100 years ago. Are there relevant echoes of current feelings and situations?

How does this novel, paired with *The Paris Wife*, rate as an introduction to the literary lens of Ernest Hemingway?

Suggested Beginnings

1. *The Paris Wife* deals heavily with a favorite Hemingway theme: loss. Both Hemingway and Hadley suffer loss before, during, and after their marriage.

   How does this shape the Hadley that McLain portrays?

2. McLain includes so many passages that highlight damage, loss, destruction, and violence that seem to foreshadow a negative end for Hadley and Hemingway.

   Was their relationship doomed from the start? Was there ever any hope that they would make it?

3. Hadley quotes Ernest as saying that *"families can be vicious."* (p.193) His parents rejected his writing success; Hadley's sister, Fonnie, seemed to be wrapped in her own gloomy story and had little support for Hadley.

   What effect does Hemingway's viewpoint have on their own little family? Consider how his perspective became the poison which destroyed all his relationships.

4. Hadley made two mistakes: she lost Ernest's life work on the train, and she became pregnant because she forgot her birth control device.

   Were these actions deliberate or inadvertent? Were they the turning point in the demise of their marriage? Would the Hemingways have succeeded if these events had not taken place?

5. Hadley is more shy and quieter than the circle of spectacular people who surround her in Paris.

   How does she feel about herself at the beginning? Does that change, and what accounts for the change? Is the Hadley we read about at the end of the novel the same or different than the woman we meet at the beginning?

6. Sherwood Anderson was an important part of Hemingway's establishment as a writer, and yet Hemingway wrote *Torrents of Spring* as a parody of one of Anderson's novels. With his insistence that the book be published, he lost the friendships of Anderson and Gertrude Stein.

   Why did he do it? Was he right to push ahead or should he have listened to the conservative voices, including Hadley's?

7. Hadley did not seem to say very much in opposition to Ernest when he began to attack Anderson, Fitzgerald, and others. As McLain portrays her, she did not agree with him, yet she does not appear to firmly speak up.

   Consider her silence in relation to Ernest's harmful behavior. Why was Hadley not more vocal, especially when, for example, Pauline supported Ernest's *Torrents of Spring*?

8. It takes Hadley a lot of time and regret before she finally gives up on her marriage to Hemingway.

   What are the stages of self-realization that she goes through? What prevents her from understanding the situation earlier?

9. By the time Hemingway commits suicide, it has been decades since Hadley had contact with him. McLain brings this up in the pages of her epilogue.

   How does Ernest's death affect Hadley? How does Hadley's reaction affect you, as the reader?

10. Hadley is very dependent on Ernest for almost every aspect of her life, including friendships, personality, and experiences. She is shaped by his wants and needs and revolves her life around these.

    Is this particular to Hadley, the person, or to the general role of a wife in the 1920s? What were the personality characteristics that defined Hadley's life with Ernest?

    Given the freedom that women had obtained in those early years, were there traditional social constraints that counteracted the new

freedoms? Did these apply only in the United States?

How would their marriage have fared if they had remained in the U.S.?

11. Taking on the character of a real person is a very interesting and bold writing technique. Nancy Horan, who wrote a blurb for *The Paris Wife*, wrote her own book about Frank Lloyd Wright called *Loving Frank*. Also, McLain has said that her next novel will be in the same genre, a fiction memoir about the scientist Marie Curie.

What are the challenges of creating the character of a real person? How can an author make this person believable? What are the traps of such a portrayal?

12. The author intends to build suspense throughout the novel by referring to future events with hints and foreshadowing.

Consider the examples of this. How do the actual events reflect the foreshadowed intensity?

FROM THE NOVEL

Quotes

FROM THE NOVEL

Memorable Quotes From the Text of *The Paris Wife*

PAGE 3. The knee is nearly enough on its own, but there's the whole package of a man attached, tall and lean, with a lot of very dark hair and a dimple in his left cheek you could fall into. His friends call him Hemingstein, Oinbones, Bird, Nesto, Wemedge, anything they can dream up on the spot ... He seems to know everyone, and everyone seems to know the same jokes and stories. They telegraph punch lines back and forth in code, lightning fast and wisecracking. I can't keep up, but I don't mind really. Being near these happy strangers is like a powerful transfusion of good cheer.

PAGE 14. "Will you let me take you to dinner?" he said.

"Now?"

"What's stopping us?"

Kate, I thought. *Kate and Kenley and the whole drunken throng in the living room.*

"No one will even notice we're gone," he said, reading my hesitation.

"All right," I said, but slunk off like a thief to get my coat anyway. I wanted to go with him. I was dying to go, but he was so wrong about no one noticing. As we ducked out the door together, I felt Kate's green eyes flashing hotly over my back and her silent shout, *Hadley, be sensible!*
I was tired of being sensible. I didn't turn around.

PAGE 25.   My mother always preferred Fonnie, who was twenty-two months older than me ... She was obedient and bendable and good in a way my mother could easily understand and praise. I was impulsive and talkative and curious about everything—far too curious for my mother's taste ...
"What could you possibly be fit for?" she often said. "You can't keep your head out of the clouds."

PAGE 37.   His letters came crushed and strangled, full of deliciousnesss, sometimes two and three a day. I tried to be more reserved at first, vowing to write only once a week, but that fell apart immediately ... The letters were flying back and forth, but what did they mean? Kate's voice often filled my head — He likes women, all women, apparently — and I debated over whether or not I should tell her about our quickly progressing friendship. I couldn't imagine her not feeling hurt and angry; I was blatantly, willfully disregarding her advice after all. But if I confessed everything, she might give me more advice, and then I'd have to listen and perhaps act on it.

PAGE 48.   When I returned home to St. Louis, Fonnie had a long string of questions and warnings. Just who was this Ernest Hemingway, anyway? What were his prospects? What could he offer me? She'd no sooner finish this line of questioning than begin her rant about my own shortcomings ... I knew Fonnie's tactics by heart and could turn her voice off almost entirely. My own voice was harder to control, unfortunately. When I was with Ernest in Chicago I'd felt strong and capable of weathering uncertainty about the future. But outside the circle of his arms, well beyond his range and powerful physical effect on me, I was struggling.

PAGE 54.   Grace insisted on showing me a photo in an obviously much-cherished album of Marcelling and Ernest dressed alike, both in pink gingham dresses and wide-brimmed straw hats trimmed with flowers.
...

Wasn't he a beautiful baby? I suppose it was silly of me to dress him like a girl, but I was indulging a whim. It didn't hurt anyone.

Ernest rolled his eyes. "That's right, Mother. Nothing ever hurts anyone."

PAGE 65. "After I was shot, when my head was still in pretty bad shape, a very wise Italian officer told me the only thing to really do for that kind of fear was get married."

"So your wife would take care of you? That's an interesting way to think about marriage."

"I actually took it to mean that if I could take care of her — you, that is — I'd worry less about myself. But maybe it works both ways."

"I'm counting on that," I said.

PAGE 70. Kenley had introduced Ernest to Anderson in the spring, before their falling-out. Winesburg, Ohio was still fairly big news, and Ernest could hardly believe Anderson would meet with him, let alone ask to see some of his stories. Anderson had seen promise in Ernest's work and offered to help launch his career if he could ... They were just back in town when Ernest sought him out and invited the couple over to dinner. I was excited to meet them but also panicked. Our flat was so terrible, how could I possibly manage to pull it off?

PAGE 80. "It's so beautiful here it hurts," Ernest said one evening as we walked to take our evening meal at the café we now frequented on rue des Saints-Pères. "Aren't you in love with it?"

I wasn't, not yet — but I was in awe of it. To walk the best streets in Paris just then was like having the curtained doors of a surreal circus standing open so you could watch the oddity and the splendor at any hour. After the enforced austerity of the war, when the textile industry collapsed and the great couturiers nailed their doors shut, brightly colored silks now ran through the streets of Paris like water — Persian blues and greens, startling oranges and golds ... Chanel was also beginning to make her mark, and you saw splashes of sharp, geometric black amid all that color. More and more, chic meant a shingle-bob and deeply lacquered nails and impossibly long ivory cigarette holders. It also meant lean and hungry looking — but that wasn't me.

PAGE 92. "What's this now? Did you miss me, Feather Cat?"

"Too much."

"Good. I like to be missed."

I nodded into his shoulder, but part of me couldn't help wondering if it *was* good to rely on him so utterly. He admired my strength and resilience and counted on it; more than this, *I* liked feeling strong and was uncomfortable knowing that had vanished when he left. Was my happiness so completely tied to him now that I could only feel like myself when he was near?

PAGE 144. Ezra was famous for his roving affections; I expected nothing less from him. But the news about Mike Strater had thrown me, because he and Maggie looked so solid. I'd been watching and admiring them and their daughter, and stitching a fantasy about how our child — mine and Ernest's — could squeeze in naturally at ringside and change very little about our lives or Ernest's work. Now that dream was punctured. This baby was almost certainly coming, but into what?

PAGE 152. "What were you hoping she'd say?" I asked when he relayed the story to me.

"I don't know. I thought she might have some advice."

"And did she?"

"No, actually. Nothing beyond, 'Do it anyway.'"

"That's perfect advice for you. You *will* do it anyway."

"Easy for you to say. All you have to do is cut and sew baby clothes."

"That and *make* the baby, thank you very much. It's not coming out of the sky."

"Right," he said distractedly, and went back to work.

PAGE 170. Winter arrived in Toronto with snow that blew sideways and threatened to knock us over. If Paris winters were damp and gray, this was fiercely white and unremitting. The wind easily pierced our coats and blankets and found its way into every corner of our apartment, where the baby and I stayed camped against the radiator. I boiled water to keep the air moist and took to wearing Ernest's big overcoat when I nursed. I didn't take the baby out at all and hired a maid to mind him when I had to do the shopping. Ernest limped home in the evening, after dark had fallen, and looked more exhausted and run down all the time. He was good about exclaiming over the baby's new accomplishments as I reported them ... but it was hard for Ernest to take any pleasure just then.

PAGE 197. "What's she doing back?" Ernest said. "I thought we were free of that gold-plated bitch."

"Be fair!" I snapped.

"I am. I know a bitch when I see one."

I tried to ignore him. He was never going to change his mind about Kitty, no matter what I said or did. It was one of his qualities that most frustrated me, how once you had a black tick in his book, you were pretty much done for. I'd have much rather not had to fight with him about her, but I was going to see Kitty anyway.

PAGE 227. Although I initially felt uneasy around Pauline and Kitty as a pair — these fashionable, independent, and decidedly modern girls — at bottom they were both wonderfully frank and unfussy. That was why they liked me, too, they insisted, and I began to trust it.

PAGE 234. In the meantime, Pauline began coming to the sawmill for dinner several nights a week, and sometimes Ernest would meet her in one or other of the cafés. I was so relieved that the relationship felt natural and mutual. I'd never liked fighting with Ernest about Kitty, but he wouldn't budge ... Pauline brought out his kinder, more fraternal side. He began to call her Pfife, and so did I ... Together we were her adorables, her cherishables.

PAGE 258, 259. "You're in love with Pauline." I made myself meet his eyes as I said it.

His shoulders stiffened and then fell. He clenched his hands and then unclenched them, but stayed silent.

"Well?"

"Well what? I can't answer you. I won't."

"Why not if it's true?" My breath was shallow, and it was getting harder and harder to look at him, to stare him down and pretend that I was in control of anything.

"Who gives a damn what's true? There are things you shouldn't say."

"What about things you shouldn't do ... What about the promises you've made?"

"Guilt won't do it, you know. If you think you can make me feel worse than I've made myself feel, you'll have to try much harder."

"Goddamn you."

"Yes, well. That much is guaranteed, I'd wager."

PAGE 298, 299. Ernest hated to be alone and always had — but Pauline's absence had left him more than alone and very vulnerable. Within a very few days, he showed up at my door at the dinner hour. He'd just finished writing for the day and had that look behind his eyes he always got when he'd been in his head for too long and needed to talk.

"How'd the work go today, Tatie?" I asked, inviting him in.

PAGE 304. In the middle of October, Ernest came around with a copy of *The Sun Also Rises*, which had just been published in the States ... Just inside the flyleaf, the book was dedicated to Bumby and to me. He'd changed it since we separated to include my name. ...

"Look what you can do. You made this."

"It's us. It's our life."

"No, it was you from the beginning. You must have known that, writing it."

"Maybe so." He looked at the book in my hands, and then turned away to the window.

PAGE 308. There are some who said I should have fought harder or longer than I did for my marriage, but in the end fighting for a love that was already gone felt like trying to live in the ruins of a lost city. I couldn't bear it, and so I backed away — and the reason I could do it at all, the reason I was strong enough and had the legs and the heart to do it, was because Ernest had come along and changed me. He helped me see what I really was and what I could do. Now that I knew what I could bear, I would have to bear losing him.

ACKNOWLEDGEMENTS

ACKNOWLEDGEMENTS

Baker, Carlos. *Ernest Hemingway: A Life Story*. Charles Scribner's Sons, New York, 1969.

Bloom, Harold (ed). *Ernest Hemingway: Bloom's BioCritiques*. Chelsea House Publishers, Philadelphia. 2002.

Bloom, Harold (ed). *Ernest Hemingway: Bloom's Modern Critical Views*. Chelsea House Publishers, Philadelphia. 2005.

Burgess, Anthony. *Ernest Hemingway*. Thames and Hudson, Great Britain, 1978.

Diliberto, Gioia. "A Hemingway Story, and Just as Fictional." The *New York Times*, Jan. 26, 1997. www.nytimes.com/books/99/07/04/specials/hemingway-diliberto.html.

Godfrey, Laura. "In Her Own Words: Q&A With Paula McLain." Bookclub-in-a-Box, Toronto. October 2011.

Hays, Matthew. "In the shadow of (Gran)Papa." The *Globe and Mail*, Toronto. Nov. 2, 2011.

Onderdonk, Todd. "'Bitched': Feminization, Identity and the Hemingwayesque in The Sun Also Rises." Twentieth Century Literature 52.1, 2006.

Wineapple, Brenda. "A novel of Hemingway's First Marriage." The *New York Times*, March 18, 2011. www.nytimes.com/2011/03/20/books/review/book-review-the-paris-wife-by-paula-mclain.html.